A Closer Walk With Christ

Presented To: Dennis Long
By: Melanie Yates
September 25, 2004

A Prayer Journal

ISBN 0-9718985-4-5
Printed in the United States of America

I *will* call on
GOD

With these words the psalmist encourages himself to pray, remembering the Lord's promised rescue (Psalm 55:16). Think of it! The God of the universe invites us, his children, to come to him with our every thought, worry, need, thanksgiving, and, yes, even our every sin. He promises to hear, accept, comfort, help, and forgive in his Son, Jesus—his eternally appointed Savior. We access the throne room of heaven as simply and immediately as a child crying out in the night: *Daddy!*

While our heavenly Father always and most gladly accepts our spontaneous and informal prayers, God's people have also been encouraged through the ages by structured, or focused, prayer. This journal includes several, more formal prayers that Christians have valued and prayed through the centuries. They have been adapted slightly to make them more accessible to you, today's reader. Also included are blank pages for you to use in recording your own prayers, letting you connect with the faithful of other centuries.

Using Your Prayer Journal

- Jot down short sentences indicative of the prayers you pray each day.

- Write out whole prayers, particularly prayers of praise and thanksgiving, word for word; then pray them often.

- Use pages 29-32 as a prayer log. (Simply record specific requests and the Lord's answers as they come.)

- Note hymns or praise choruses that help you as you pray.

- Keep in mind others may some day read this journal; for instance, you may pass it to your children or grandchildren so they can read your testimony of our Savior's faithfulness to you.

- Use the P.R.A.Y. acronym as you approach the throne of grace.

Praise

Our Lord invites us to enter his presence with praise and thanksgiving (Psalm 100:4), not because he needs our prayers but because of *our* need. We need to praise him! As we praise, we remind ourselves of God's goodness, his power, his wisdom, and his unchanging love and mercy for us in Jesus, our Savior. Praise helps us recall who God is and what he is already doing in our lives.

Repent

Our sin separates us from God. It erects barriers to prayers prayed in faith (Isaiah 59:2). When we confess our sins, God forgives them freely because of his Son's sacrifice on the cross. To repent means to turn away from our sins and turn back to God. When we repent we receive not only his pardon, but also his power to obey.

Ask

No request is too small. None is too big. Our Lord cares about everything that concerns or troubles us. When we pray, we trust him to answer, doing what is the very best for us and for those we love (Romans 8:28).

Yield

As the Holy Spirit works trust into our hearts, we yield our lives, our desires, and our circumstances to God's care. We believe his goodness and rely on his power to live in alignment with his commands.

Lord, we do not know what we
ought to ask of you.
You and you alone know what we need.
You love us better than we know how
to love ourselves.

O Father,
give to us, your children,
that for which we do not know how to ask.
We would have no other desire
than to do your will.

Teach us to pray.
Pray yourself in us.
For Christ's sake. Amen

~from France
circa 1650; adapted

Praise

_____

_____

_____

_____

_____

Repent

_____

_____

_____

_____

_____

Ask

_____

_____

_____

_____

_____

Yield

The LORD is good.
His unfailing love con-
tinues forever, and his
faithfulness continues to
each generation.
~Psalm 100:5

Praise _____

_____

_____

_____

_____

_____

Repent _____

_____

_____

_____

_____

_____

_____

Ask _____

_____

_____

_____

_____

_____

Yield _____

_____

_____

_____

_____

_____

_____

_____

_____

_____

How we praise God, the Father of our Lord Jesus Christ, who has blessed us with every spiritual blessing in the heavenly realms because we belong to Christ. Long ago, even before he made the world, God loved us and chose us in Christ to be holy and without fault in his eyes.
~ Ephesians 1:3-4

Praise _____

_____
_____
_____
_____
_____

Repent _____

_____
_____
_____
_____
_____

Ask _____

_____
_____
_____
_____
_____

Yield _____

All honor to the God and Father of our Lord Jesus Christ, for it is by his boundless mercy that God has given us the privilege of being born again. Now we live with a wonderful expectation because Jesus Christ rose again from the dead.
~ 1 Peter 1:3

Praise _____

_____

_____

_____

_____

Repent _____

_____

_____

_____

_____

Ask _____

_____

_____

_____

_____

Yield _____

_____

_____

_____

_____

The LORD is kind and merciful, slow to get angry, full of unfailing love. The LORD is good to everyone. He showers compassion on all his creation.
~ Psalm 145:8-9

O God,
the Father of our Lord
and Savior, Jesus Christ,
you ride upon the Cherubim
and are glorified by the Seraphim.
Thousands upon thousands,
ten thousand upon ten thousand
angels and archangels serve you!
Sanctify us, O Lord,
body, soul, and spirit.
Cast out every evil thought
or desire, all envy and pride,
all worry and deceit, all anger and
memory of past injuries, and
every other thing contrary to your holy will.
Grant us with freedom, with a
pure heart, and with a humble soul boldly
to call upon you,
our holy God and Father. Amen.

~from the first century church;
adapted

Praise _____

_____
_____
_____
_____
_____

Repent _____

_____
_____
_____
_____
_____

Ask _____

_____
_____
_____
_____
_____

Yield _____

... the LORD says, "Turn
to me now, while there
is time! Give me your
hearts. Come with fast-
ing, weeping, and
mourning. Don't tear
your clothing in your
grief; instead, tear your
hearts." Return to the
LORD your God, for he
is gracious and merciful.
~ Joel 2:12-13a

Praise _____

_____

_____

_____

_____

_____

Repent _____

_____

_____

_____

_____

_____

Ask _____

_____

_____

_____

_____

Yield _____

... forgive us our sins,
just as we have forgiv-
en those who have
sinned against us. And
don't let us yield to
temptation, but deliver
us from the evil one.
~ Matthew 6:12-13

Praise _____

_____

_____

_____

_____

Repent _____

_____

_____

_____

_____

Ask _____

_____

_____

_____

_____

Yield _____

_____

_____

_____

People who cover over their sins will not prosper. But if they confess and forsake them, they will receive mercy.

~ Proverbs 28:13

Praise

_____

_____

_____

_____

Repent

_____

_____

_____

_____

Ask

_____

_____

_____

_____

Yield

... I am writing to you so that you will not sin. But if you do sin, there is someone to plead for you before the Father. He is Jesus Christ, the one who pleases God completely. He is the sacrifice for our sins. He takes away not only our sins but the sins of all the world.

~ 1 John 2:1-2

Praise

_____

_____

_____

_____

_____

Repent

_____

_____

_____

_____

_____

Ask

_____

_____

_____

_____

_____

Yield

Praise the LORD, I tell myself, and never forget the good things he does for me. He forgives all my sins and heals all my diseases. He ransoms me from death and surrounds me with love and tender mercies.
~ Psalm 103:2-4

Almighty God,
we humbly acknowledge our many sins
against you in thought and deed.
We have neglected to do good when you,
in love, have given us many opportunities.
We have fallen for temptations from
which you were eager
to guard us. We have tried to please people
rather than seeking to honor you.
We have thought too little about how to help others
and too much about our own pleasures.
Holy Father, you are merciful and gracious to those
who turn to you. Lord Jesus, you are the Lamb of God
who takes away the sin of the world. Holy Spirit,
you help us in our weakness. Receive our confession
and give us true repentance and trust in you.
Forgive our sins, though many and serious, and
give us grace to live for
the glory of your great Name. Amen.

~from England,
circa 1825; adapted

Praise _____

_____

_____

_____

_____

_____

Repent _____

_____

_____

_____

_____

_____

Ask _____

_____

_____

_____

_____

_____

Yield _____

_____

_____

_____

I will answer them
before they even call to
me. While they are still
talking to me about
their needs, I will go
ahead and answer
their prayers!
~ Isaiah 65:24

Praise _____

_____

_____

_____

_____

_____

Repent _____

_____

_____

_____

_____

_____

Ask _____

_____

_____

_____

_____

_____

Yield _____

**Answer me when I call,
O God who declares
me innocent. Take
away my distress.
Have mercy on me and
hear my prayer.**
~ Psalm 4:1

Praise _____

_____

_____

_____

_____

_____

Repent _____

_____

_____

_____

_____

_____

Ask _____

_____

_____

_____

_____

_____

Yield _____

_____

_____

_____

_____

... [Jesus] went up into the hills by himself to pray.

~ Mark 6:46

Praise _____

_____
_____
_____
_____
_____

Repent _____

_____
_____
_____
_____
_____

Ask _____

_____
_____
_____
_____
_____

Yield _____

[Jesus said,] "Keep on asking, and you will be given what you ask for. Keep on looking, and you will find. Keep on knocking, and the door will be opened."
~ Matthew 7:7

Praise _____

_____
_____
_____
_____

Repent _____

_____
_____
_____
_____

Ask _____

_____
_____
_____
_____

Yield _____

_____
_____
_____
_____
_____
_____
_____
_____
_____

One day Jesus told his disciples a story to illustrate their need for constant prayer and to show them that they must never give up.
~ Luke 18:1

(Ed. Note: You may want to read the story Jesus told. See Luke.)

Grant, O Lord,
that we may
live in your fear,
die in your favor,
rest in your peace,
rise in your power, and
reign in your glory,
for the sake of your Son,
Jesus Christ, our Lord. Amen.

~from England,
1573; adapted

Praise

_____

_____

_____

_____

_____

_____

Repent

_____

_____

_____

_____

_____

_____

Ask

_____

_____

_____

_____

_____

_____

Yield

_____

_____

_____

_____

"The will of the LORD be done."

~ Acts 21:14b

Praise _____

_____

_____

_____

_____

_____

Repent _____

_____

_____

_____

_____

_____

Ask _____

_____

_____

_____

_____

_____

Yield _____

May your Kingdom come soon. May your Will be done here on earth, just as it is in heaven.
~ Matthew 6:10

Praise _____

_____

_____

_____

_____

_____

Repent _____

_____

_____

_____

_____

_____

Ask _____

_____

_____

_____

_____

_____

Yield _____

_____

_____

_____

_____

_____

_____

_____

> ... let God transform you into a new person by changing the way you think. Then you will know what God wants you to do, and you will know how good and pleasing and perfect his will really is.
> ~ Romans 12:2

Praise

_____

_____

_____

_____

_____

Repent

_____

_____

_____

_____

_____

Ask

_____

_____

_____

_____

_____

Yield

God is working in you, giving you the desire to obey him and the power to do what pleases him.
~ Philippians 2:13

Praise _____

_____

_____

_____

_____

_____

Repent _____

_____

_____

_____

_____

Ask _____

_____

_____

_____

_____

Yield _____

_____

_____

_____

_____

> No discipline is enjoyable while it is happening – it is painful! But afterward there will be a quiet harvest of right living for those who are trained in this way.
> ~ Hebrews 12:11

Merciful Lord,
the Comforter and Teacher of your faithful people,
increase in your church those desires
that you have given.
Confirm the hearts of those who
hope in you by enabling us to understand
the depth of your promises.
Grant that all of your adopted sons and
daughters may even now see with eyes of faith
and await in patience the light which you
have not yet revealed.
Through Jesus Christ, our Lord. Amen.

~St. Ambrose,
circa 340; adapted

Prayer Log

I pray that you will begin to understand the incredible greatness of his power for us who believe him.

~Ephesians 1:19

My Request	Date of Request	God's Response	Date of Reponse

Prayer Log

"Pray that you will not be overcome by temptation."

~Luke 22:40

My Request	Date of Request	God's Response	Date of Reponse

Prayer Log

"Your prayers and gifts to the poor have not gone unnoticed by God!"

~Acts 10:4

My Request	Date of Request	God's Response	Date of Reponse

Prayer Log

May you overflow with hope through the power of the Holy Spirit.

~ Romans 15:13

My Request	Date of Request	God's Response	Date of Reponse